SING with all my Soul

Edited by William Llewellyn

The Royal School of Church Music

COPYRIGHT INFORMATION AND ACKNOWLEDGEMENTS

Designed by John Sansom.
Originated by Jonathan English
Printed by Halstan & Co. Ltd., Amersham, Bucks.

PREFACE

Another hymnbook? Let me explain!

I have frequently been asked whether the RSCM could provide a collection of the best words and music in the worship-song repertoire. This book is an attempt to satisfy this request.

But it is more than that. Without adding musical ideas which are alien to the melodies, we have provided material for choirs and instruments which enriches without detracting from the essential popular appeal of the original songs. We have also provided in some instances keyboard accompaniments which those without improvisational skills will find lie under the hands in a more friendly way.

A quick glance through any hymnbook will provide ample evidence to show that many of the finest tunes of the past four centuries have originated in the popular tradition. Vaughan Williams recognized this when he included folk melodies in The English Hymnal way back in 1906. But he was not the first to do this. Nor is the discovery of fine melody something confined to the study of past ages.

It becomes increasingly clear that the present age is one of great creative activity in the popular folk tradition. This book provides fine examples of spontaneous and memorable tunes which have come to life in recent years. They encompass a wide range of emotions from quiet devotion to exuberant, uncomplicated joy. We hope choirs, congregations and instrumentalists will find here new ideas to refresh and deepen the worship in their churches.

We would like to thank all the musicians who have willingly found time to make a contribution to this collection.

Norman Warren, Archdeacon of Rochester, has given advice at all stages of preparation. The bulk of the editorial and musical work has been undertaken by William Llewellyn, a task which involved the expenditure of much time and energy. Jonathan English has worked painstakingly to set the music. The RSCM is extremely grateful to all who have helped to bring this book to birth.

Harry Bramma.
Director RSCM.

CONTENTS

1. A gift from heav'n above (The Father's Gift)

Words: John Sanders

Music: John Sanders

2. *Alleluia, alleluia, give thanks*

Words: Don Fishel

Music: Don Fishel
Arranged: Patrick Hawes

3. A new commandment

Words: from John 13

Music: Unknown
Arranged: Paul Leddington Wright

4. At your feet we fall

Words: Dave Fellingham

Music: Dave Fellingham
Arranged: Norman Warren

1. At your feet we fall,_____ might-y ris - en Lord,_____ as we
2. There we see you stand,_____ might-y ris - en Lord,_____ clothed in
3. Like the shi - ning sun_____ in its noon - day strength,_____ we now

come be - fore your throne to wor-ship you!_____ By your Spi - rit's power_____ you now
gar-ments pure and ho - ly, shi - ning bright;_____ eyes of flash-ing fire,_____ feet like
see the glo - ry of your won-drous face:_____ once that face was marred,_____ now you're

draw our hearts,____ and we hear___ your voice in tri - umph ring-ing clear:_____
burn-ished bronze,____ and the sound___ of ma - ny wa - ters is your voice._____
glo - ri - fied;____ and your words,like a two-edged sword, have might-y power._____

5. Be still, for the presence of the Lord

Words: Dave Evans (based on Exodus 3: 1-6)

Music: Dave Evans
Arranged: Martin How

In Him no sin is found, we stand on Ho - ly ground. Be still, for the
How awe-some is the sight, our ra - diant King of light! Be still, for the
No work too hard for Him, in faith re - ceive from Him; Be still, for the

pre - sence of the Lord, the Ho - ly One is here. *p* 2. Be still, for the
glo - ry of the Lord is shin - ing all a - round. *mf* 3. Be still, for the
pow - er of the Lord is mov - ing in this place.

6. Bind us together, Lord

Words: Bernard Gillman

Music: Bernard Gillman
Arranged: Norman Warre
Descant: William Llewellyr

1. There—— is on - ly one God: there—— is on - ly one King,
2. Made for the glo - ry of God, pur - chased by his pre - cious Son,
3. You are the fami - ly of God, you are the pro - mise di - vine,

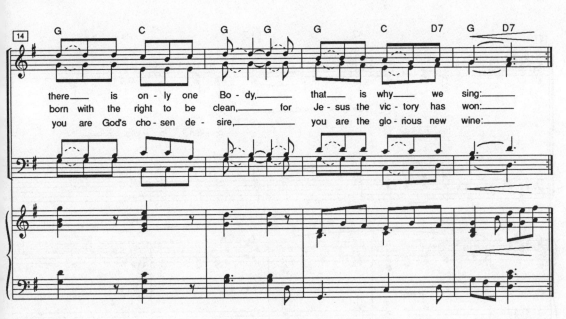

there—— is on - ly one Bo - dy,—— that—— is why—— we sing:
born with the right to be clean,—— for Je - sus the vic - tory has won:
you are God's cho - sen de - sire,—— you are the glo - rious new wine:

7. Broken for me, broken for you (i)

Words: Janet Lunt

Music: Janet Lunt
Arranged: Martin How

8. Broken for me, broken for you (ii)

Words: Janet Lunt

Music: John Sanders

9. Day by day

Words: Richard of Chichester

Music: Norman Warren
Arranged: Harry Bramma

Org. Ped (ad lib)

10. Be still, and know that I am God

Words: Unknown (from Psalm 46 v. 10)

Music: Unknown
Arranged: Martin How

11. Father, we adore you

Words: Terrye Coelho

Music: Terrye Coelho
Arranged: William Llewellyn

12. *From heaven you came* *(The Servant King)*

Words: Graham Kendrick

Music: Graham Kendrick
Arranged: Jeremy Thurlow

Organ

All voices

1. From heaven you came, help-less Babe — en-tered our world, your glo-ry veiled,
2. There in the gar-den of tears, my hea-vy load he chose to bear;
3. Come, see his hands and his feet, the scars that speak of sac-ri-fice,
4. So let us learn how to serve, and in our lives en-throne— him,

not to be served but to serve, and give your life that we might
his heart with sor-row was torn, 'Yet not my will, but yours,' he
hands that flung stars in-to space to cru-el nails sur-rend -
each oth-er's needs to pre-fer — for it is Christ we're serv -

S./A./Congregation

[13] Chorus

live.
said.
—ered.
—ing.

This is our God — the ser-vant king. He calls us now to fol-low him, to bring our

T./B.

[18]

lives as a dai-ly of-fer-ing of wor-ship to the ser-vant king. king.

Verse 3 : optional setting for choir/organ only (guitar silent)

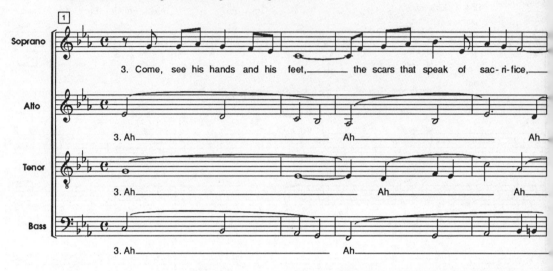

Soprano: 3. Come, see his hands and his feet,_____ the scars that speak of sac-ri-fice,_____

Alto: 3. Ah_____ Ah_____ Ah____

Tenor: 3. Ah_____ Ah_____ Ah____

Bass: 3. Ah_____ Ah____

All   to Chorus
Bar 14

Soprano: _hands that flung stars in-to space,_____ to cru-el nails sur - rend - ered._____ This is our

Alto: _____ Ah_____ Ah_____ This is our

Tenor: _____ Ah_____ Ah_____ This is our

Bass: _____ Ah_____ This is our

13. *Father, we love you*

Words: Donna Adkins

Music: Donna Adkins
Arranged: Norman Warren
Descant: William Llewellyn

14. *God forgave my sin (Freely, freely)*

Words: Carol Owens

Music: Carol Owens
Arranged: David Meacoc

15. God has spoken

Words: Willard Jabusch

Music: Israeli folk melody
Arranged: William Llewellyn

God has spo - ken to his peo - ple, Al - le - lu - ia,

and his words are words of wis - dom, Al - le - lu - ia.

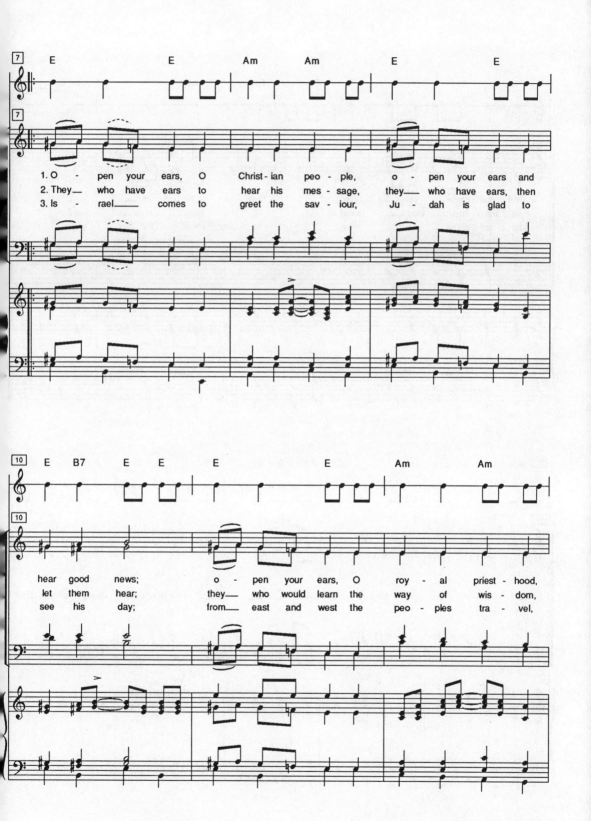

1. O - pen your ears, O Christ - ian peo - ple, o - pen your ears and
2. They_ who have ears to hear his mes - sage, they_ who have ears, then
3. Is - rael_ comes to greet the sav - iour, Ju - dah is glad to

hear good news; o - pen your ears, O roy - al priest - hood,
let them hear; they_ who would learn the way of wis - dom,
see his day; from_ east and west the peo - ples tra - vel,

16. God is good

Words: Graham Kendrick

Music: Graham Kendrick
Arranged: William Llewellyn

pause only if finishing here

we sing and shout__ it,__ God is good — we know it's true!

pause only if finishing here

Optional choir ending

God is good!_____

Optional choir ending

17. Hallelujah, my Father

Words: Tim Cullen

Music: Tim Cullen
Arranged: Norman Warren
Keyboard: William Llewellyn

Descant: Hal-le - lu-jah, Hal-le - lu - jah, Hal-le - lu - jah to the

Soprano/Alto/Congregation: Hal-le - lu - jah, my Fa - ther,— for— giv-ing us your

Son;— Send-ing him in-to the world to be giv - en up for us.—

Son; Send-ing him— in - to the world— to be giv-en up for us.—

18. Holy, holy, holy

Words: Jimmy Owens

Music: Jimmy Owens
Arranged: William Llewellyn

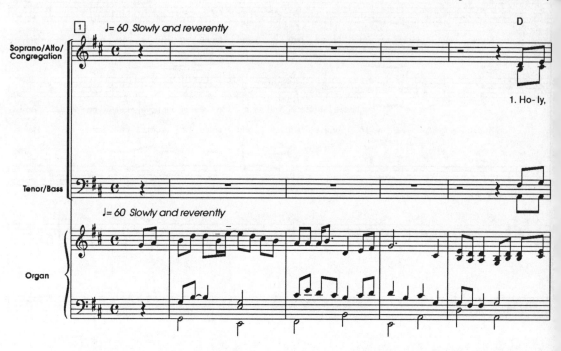

-lu - jah! Hal-le - lu - jah! And we lift our hearts be-fore___ you as a to-ken of our love, Hal-le-

-lu-jah! Hal - le - lu - jah! Hal - le - lu - jah!_____

19. I was glad

Words: Norman Warren

Music: Norman Warren
Arranged: Martin How

20. Holy, holy, holy is the Lord

Words: from Revelation 4

Music: Unknown
Arranged: Norman Warren

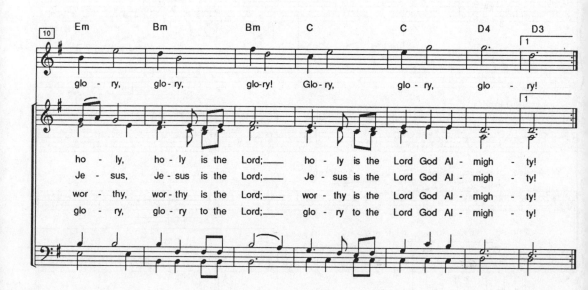

21. Holy, holy, holy, the Lord God is holy

Words: Norman Warren

Music: Norman Warren
Descant: William Llewellyn

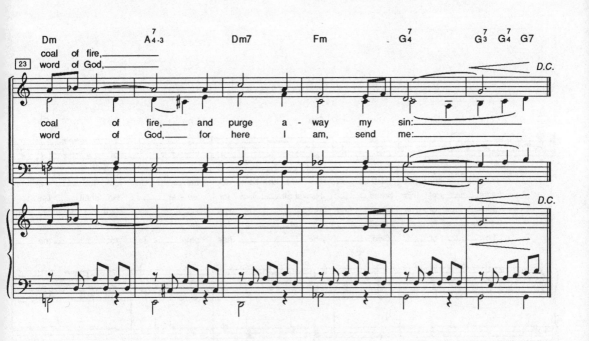

22. *I am the Bread of Life*

Words: S. Suzanne Toolan

Music: S. Suzanne Toolan
Arranged: Jeremy Thurlow

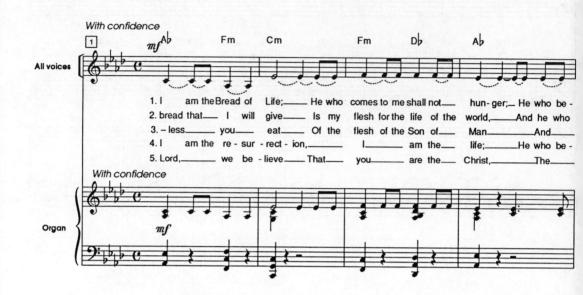

1. I am the Bread of Life;— He who comes to me shall not— hun- ger;— He who be -
2. bread that— I will give— Is my flesh for the life of the world,—And he who
3. -less— you— eat Of the flesh of the Son of— Man— And—
4. I am the re - sur - rect - ion,— I— am the— life;—He who be -
5. Lord,— we be - lieve— That— you— are the— Christ,—The

- lieves in me shall not thirst;— No one can come to me— Un -less the— Fa- ther
eats— of this bread,— He shall— live for ev- er,— He shall— live for
drink— of His blood, And drink— of His blood,— You shall not have life with-
- lieves— in— me, Ev - en— if he die,— He shall— live for
Son— of— God,— who— has come— in - to— the—

23. *Jesus is King*

Words: Wendy Churchill

Music: Wendy Churchill
Arranged: Norman Warren
Descants: William Llewellyn

1. Je - sus is king, and we will ex - tol him, give him the
2. We have a hope that is stead - fast and cer - tain, gone through the
3. We come to him, our Priest and A - pos - tle, clothed in his
4. 'O Ho - ly One, our hearts do a - dore you; thrilled with your

good - ness we give you our praise!' An - gels in light with wor - ship sur -
cur - tain and touch - ing the throne; we have a Priest who is there in - ter -
glo - ry, and bear - ing his name, lay - ing our lives with glad - ness be -
good - ness we give you our praise!' An - gels in light with wor - ship sur -

round him, Je - sus, our Sav - iour, for ev - er the same.

hea - vens Word of the Fa - ther, ex - alt - ed for us.
-ced - ing, pour - ing his grace on our lives day by day.
-fore him, filled with his Spi - rit, we wor - ship the King.
round him, Je - sus, our Sav - iour, for ev - er the same.

24. Jesus, stand among us

Words: Graham Kendrick

Music: Graham Kendrick
Arranged: Noël Tredinnick

our— fear.————————
—way———

—way— our— fear.————————
—way—

25. Jesus, I worship you

Words: Norman Warren

Music: Norman Warren

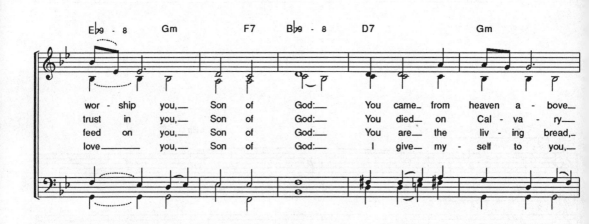

26. Jubilate, everybody

Words: Fred Dunn from Psalm 100 after Michael Perry

Music: Fred Dunn (1907 - 79)
Arranged: William Llewellyn

come be-fore his— pre-sence sing-ing;— en-ter now— his— courts with praise.

come be-fore his pre-sence sing - ing; en-ter now— his— courts with praise.

S./A./
Congregation
For the Lord our— God is gra-cious,— and his mer-cy's ev-er-last-ing.

For the Lord our God is gra - cious, and his mer-cy's ev-er-last-ing.

T./B.

27. Lord, have mercy on us

Words: Graham Kendrick

Music: Graham Kendrick
Arranged: Norman Warren

Hum- bly we bow___ and call up-on you now,___ O___ Lord,_____ have

mer- cy___ on___ us.____ O us.____

28. *Lord, the light of your love (Shine, Jesus, shine)*

Words: Graham Kendrick

Music: Graham Kendrick
Arranged: William Llewellyn

1. Lord, the light of Your love is shin-ing, In the midst of the dark-ness, shin-ing: Je-sus, Light of the World, shine up-on—— us, Set us free by the truth you now bring—— us—
2. Lord, I come to Your awe-some pres-ence, From the sha-dows in-to Your ra-diance; By your blood I may en-ter your bright-ness: Search me, try me, con-sume all my dark-ness—
3. As we gaze on Your king-ly bright-ness, So our fa-ces dis-play Your like-ness, Ev-er chang-ing from glo-ry to glo-ry: Mir-rored here, may our lives tell Your sto-ry—

29. Spirit of the living God

Words: Daniel Iverson (verse 1)
Michael Baughen (verse 2)

Music: Daniel Iverson
Arranged: Paul Leddington Wright

30. Majesty

Words: Jack Hayford

Music: Jack Hayford
Arranged: David Meacock

31. *Make me a channel*

Words: Based on a traditional prayer

Melody: Sebastian Temp[le]
Arranged: William Llewe[llyn]

32. May the fragrance of Jesus

Words: Graham Kendrick

Music: Graham Kendrick
Arranged: William Llewellyn

1. May the fra-grance of Je-sus fill this place.
2. May the glo-ry of Je-sus fill his church.
3. May the beau-ty of Je-sus fill my life.

Love - ly fra-grance of Je sus Ris - ing from the sa - cri - fice of
Ra - diant glo - ry of Je sus Shi - ning from our fa - ces
Per - fect beau - ty of Je sus Fill my thoughts, my words, my deeds. My

place.
church.
life.

lives laid down in a-dor-a - tion.
As we gaze in a-dor-a - tion.
all I give in a-dor-a - tion.

33. Meekness and majesty (This is your God)

Words: Graham Kendrick

Music: Graham Kendrick
Arranged: William Llewellyn

34. 'Moses, I know you're the man'

Words: Estelle White

Music: Estelle White
Arranged: William Llewellyn

1. 'Mos - es, I know you're the man,' the Lord said.
2. 'Don't get too set in your ways,' the Lord said.
3. 'No mat - ter what you may do,' the Lord said.
4. 'Look at the birds in the air,' the Lord said.
5. 'Fox - es have pla - ces to go,' the Lord said.

'You're going to work out my plan,' the Lord said. 'Lead all the Is - rael - ites
'Each step is on - ly a phase,' the Lord said. 'I'll go be - fore you and
'I shall be faith - ful and true,' the Lord said. 'My love will strength - en you
'They fly un - ham - pered by care,' the Lord said. 'You will move eas - i - er
'But I've no home here be - low,' the Lord said. 'So if you want to be

out of sla - ver - y, And I shall make them a wan - der - ing
I shall be a sign To guide my tra - vel - ling, wan - der - ing
as you go a - long, For you're my tra - vel - ling, wan - der - ing
if you're tra - velling light, For you're a wan - der - ing, va - ga - bond
with me all your days, Keep up the mov - ing and tra - vel - ling

35. O Holy Spirit

Words: Norman Warren

Music: Norman Warren
Arranged: Martin How

36. *O let the Son of God enfold you (Spirit Song)*

Words: John Wimber

Music: John Wimber
Arranged: Norman Warren
Keyboard: William Llewellyn

Fm   Bb7 Cm Bb7 Eb   Eb7 Db Eb7

fill your heart and sa-tis-fy your soul._____ O let Him
hands in sweet sur-ren-der to His name._____ O give Him

Ab   Fm   Bb Gm Ab4-3

dove, will des-
pain, and you'll

have the things that hold you and His Spi- rit, like a dove, will des -
all your tears and sad- ness, give Him all your years of pain, and you'll

37. Restore, O Lord

Words: Graham Kendrick/Chris Rolinson

Music: Graham Kendrick/Chris Rolinson
Arranged: Norman Warren

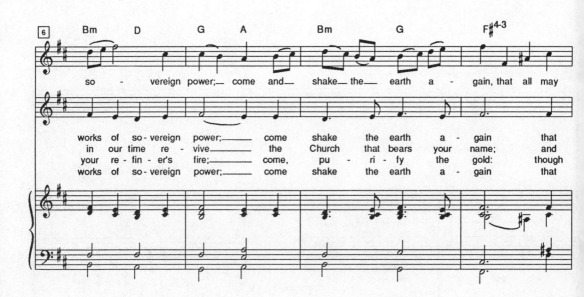

38. Seek ye first the kingdom of God

Words: Karen Lafferty from Matthew 6: 33, 7:7 and Deuteronomy 8:3

Music: Karen Lafferty
Arranged: William Llewellyn

39. There is a Redeemer

Words: Melody Green

Music: Melody Green
Arranged: Norman Warren

40. Sing alleluia to the Lord

Words: Linda Stassen

Music: Linda Stassen
Arranged: William Llewellyn

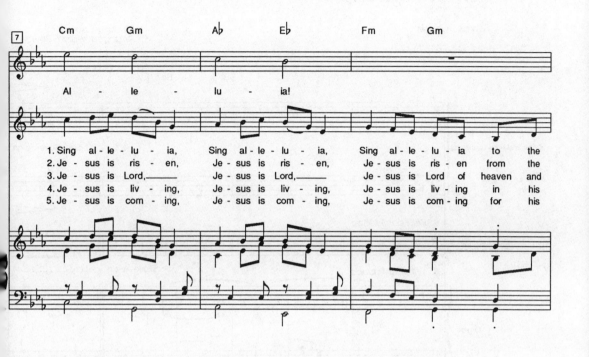

Alleluia!

1. Sing al-le-lu-ia, Sing al-le-lu-ia, Sing al-le-lu-ia to the
2. Je-sus is ris-en, Je-sus is ris-en, Je-sus is ris-en from the
3. Je-sus is Lord,___ Je-sus is Lord,___ Je-sus is Lord of heaven and
4. Je-sus is liv-ing, Je-sus is liv-ing, Je-sus is liv-ing in his
5. Je-sus is com-ing, Je-sus is com-ing, Je-sus is com-ing for his

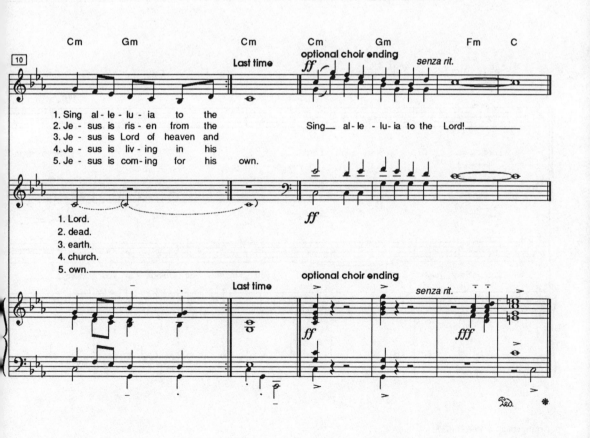

1. Sing al-le-lu-ia to the
2. Je-sus is ris-en from the
3. Je-sus is Lord of heaven and
4. Je-sus is liv-ing in his
5. Je-sus is com-ing for his own.

Sing___ al-le-lu-ia to the Lord!___

1. Lord.
2. dead.
3. earth.
4. church.
5. own.___

41. Sovereign Lord

Words: Unknown

Music: Unknown
Arranged: William Llewellyn

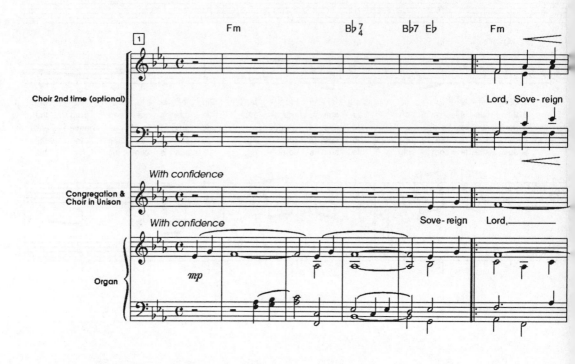

42. Such love

Words: Graham Kendrick

Music: Graham Kendrick
Arranged: William Llewellyn

Such love, paying the debt I owe.
Such love, showing me holiness. O
Such love, fountain of life to me.

Jesus, such love.

2. Such love.
3. Such love.

43. Take this bread (i)

Words: Barry McGuire

Music: Barry McGuire
Arranged: Jeremy Thurlow

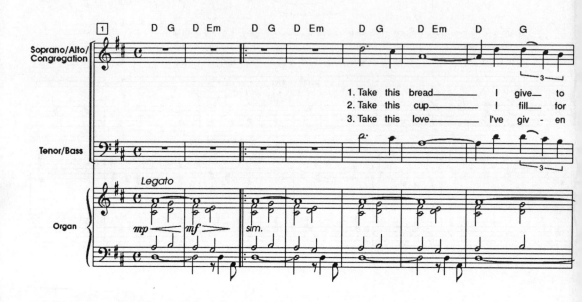

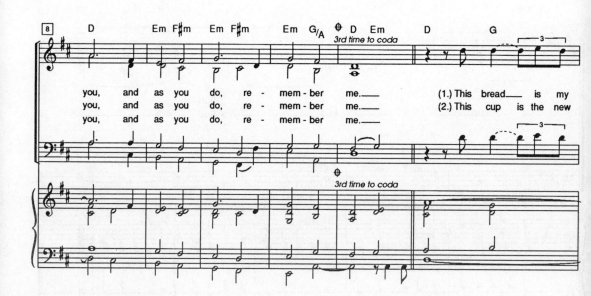

44. *Take this bread (ii)*

Words: Barry McGuire

Music: John Sanders

45. Thank you, Jesus

Words: Unknown

Music: Unknown
Arranged: Norman Warren
Keyboard: William Llewellyn

46. Thank you, Lord

Words: Norman Warren

Music: Norman Warren
Arranged: Martin How

47. We are here to praise you

Words: Graham Kendrick

Music: Graham Kendrick
Arranged: Norman Warren
Keyboard: William Llewellyn

give you _____ the best that we can bring. _____ Lord, it is our

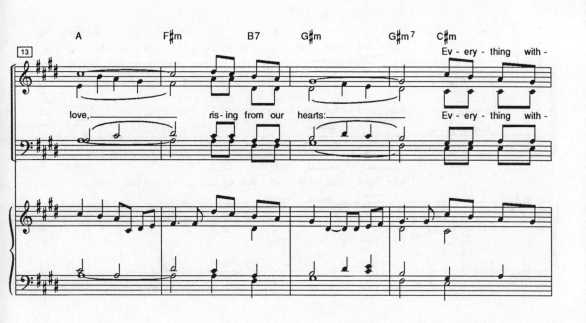

love, _____ ris-ing from our hearts: _____ Ev-ery-thing with-

48. *When I look into your Holiness*

Words: Wayne and Cathy Perrin

Music: Wayne and Cathy Perrin
Arranged: Jeremy Thurlow

I wor-ship You,_____ I wor-ship You._____ The rea-son I live___

_ is to wor-ship You._____ I wor-ship _ is to wor-ship You._____

49. With my heart I worship you

Words: Norman Warren

Music: Norman Warren
Descant: William Llewel

50. You are the King of glory

Words: Mavis Ford

Music: Mavis Ford
Arranged: William Llewellyn

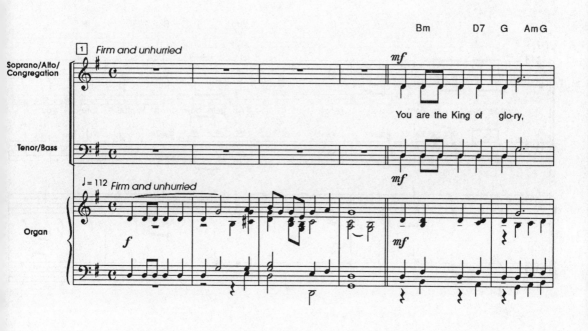

51. *You have changed my sadness*

Words: Norman Warren (*from Psalm 30*)

Music: Norman Warren
Descants: William Llewellyn

S. T.
A. B.

You have ta - ken a - way my sor - row and sur - round - ed me with joy;____
Lord, you are____ my God,____ I will give you thanks for ev - er; so____

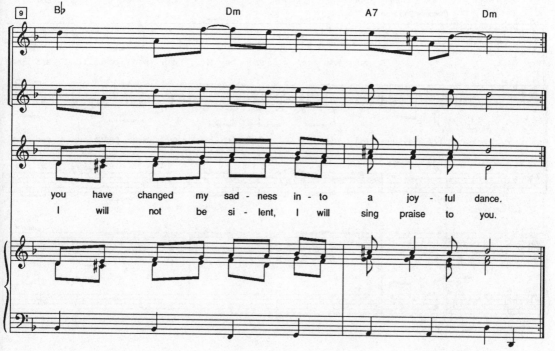

you have changed my sad - ness in - to a joy - ful dance.
I will not be si - lent, I will sing praise to you.

52. You shall go out with joy (The trees of the field)

Words: Stuart Dauermann from Isaiah 55:12

Music: Steffi Geiser Rubin
Arranged: David Meacock

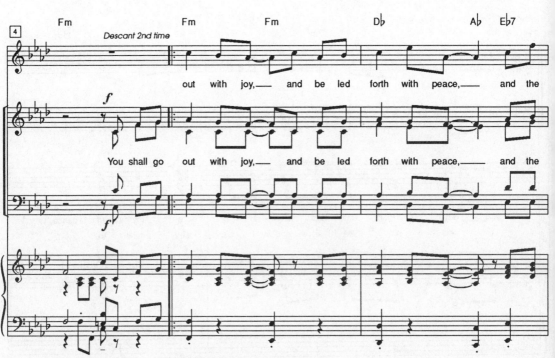

trees of the field shall clap their hands, and the trees of the field shall

trees of the field shall clap their hands, and the trees of the field shall

clap their hands, and the trees of the field shall clap their hands, and

clap their hands, and the trees of the field shall clap their hands, and

PERFORMANCE SUGGESTIONS

A General Note for Conductors, Singers and Instrumentalists

These Worship Songs have been arranged for churches with singers who may wish to sing anything from unison to full SATB. The arrangements will work with whatever resources are available, and will benefit from the initiative and imagination of the performers themselves; for instance, in a number of songs it is possible for the Soprano part to be sung and the ATB part hummed, perhaps in a final repeat of the opening verse.

There are instrumental opportunities in many of the parts marked "Descant". Flutes, oboes, clarinets (B flat descant parts will be available), violins, chime bars and glockenspiels playing these will add colour and interest. In cases where two descants are printed it is possible to have on or both sung, one or both played, or you may combine singing and playing.

If you have percussion instruments, by all means use them: you can devise your own rhythms for many of the pieces.

The keyboard parts have been labelled "Organ", but Piano or other Keyboard will work perfectly well. In some cases organists and pianists may wish to make their own adjustments. In Songs with a very strong bass rhythm, staccato bass notes will help greatly.

A Note about Syncopation

Some of the Songs have syncopated rhythms to be sung or played. Syncopation is not the mysterious affair which some people imagine it to be. The principle of arriving on a note on a stressed weak beat and holding that note through the next strong one needs only simple precision and a clear basic beat to be effective. A useful method of practising is to start by ignoring the tie and replaying the note, checking that everything is exactly in time. Now replace the tie, and stress the note as you arrive on it; adjust the weight of the sound in rehearsal until you are satisfied that it is appropriate.

Performance Notes

1 **A gift from heav'n above (*The Father's Gift*)**
Reflective, flowing singing.

3 **A new commandment**
The words of Christ speak for themselves: if sung by a choir, remember that each part is not only harmony, but a melody with a life of its own.

2 **Alleluia, alleluia, give thanks**
A song of praise, cheerful, rhythmic and resonant. The addition of the descant in the last chorus can help to make a fine climax.

4 **At your feet we fall**
We see Christ living and in Majesty. Sing with firmness, filling words like "mighty", "triumph", "shining" and "wondrous" with resonant sound.

10 **Be still, and know that I am God**
Always gentle with an awareness of God's presence. The descants may be used, for example, one in verse 2, followed by the other in verse 3. The opening organ bars could be played on wind or string instruments.

5 **Be still, for the presence of the Lord**
Long, sustained phrases, warm, quiet singing, and very careful phrase endings will enhance the calmness this song so beautifully evokes. Words like "shining" can be illuminated, always with devotion.

6 **Bind us together, Lord**
Lilting and gentle. There must always be time for clarity in the words, and the chords on "God" and "King" can glow.

7 **Broken for me, broken for you (i)**
The refrain "Broken for you" is thoughtful: Christ's invitations in verses 2, 3 and 4 can sound full without spoiling the devotional aspect of the song.

8 **Broken for me, broken for you (ii)**
Slow, with the quavers very expressively sung. The rise and fall of the music gives opportunities for beautiful and thoughtful singing.

9 **Day by day**
Two gentle beats in a bar, with the words "see", "love", "follow" and the rhyming words "clearly", "dearly" and "nearly" all given special attention.

11 **Father, we adore you**
This three-part round works in unison or harmony. The accompanist may choose to play the choir harmonies for the first verse, and the lower stave harmonies for subsequent verses. There is an opportunity for some simple rhythmic improvisation by the player. You may organise the round as you choose: it can grow and finish strongly, or it can become loud in the middle and fade away, finishing very softly with the last group of singers. The choir may be split into three groups which may be placed in different parts of the church. The last two bars of the descant may be sung three times to finish with the third group.

13 Father, we love you
Each verse starts quietly and grows in volume and resonance to its climax.

12 From heaven you came, helpless babe
(*The Servant King*)
Thoughtful singing of the words, never rushed, will carry the meaning of the contrast between servant and King. The optional setting of verse 3 may have humming instead of "Ah", and may be with or without organ until the refrain.

14 God forgave my sin *(Freely, freely)*
The descant may be used in each chorus, or reserved until the second verse. In Bar 29 the Bass C should be firm to provide a gentle additional impulse. *The arranger offers a colourful alternative in Bar 35 of two B naturals in the tenor part, followed by B flat on the third beat, clashing discreetly with the descant!* The speed must be such that the quavers (in Bars 16 - 20, for example) never sound hurried.

15 God has spoken
If you enjoy Hungarian Gipsy bands, then this is for you! The Bass must have precisely timed, striding, staccato notes. These, together with the percussion part (which can be played on almost any instrument) provide the driving force for the song. The optional ending for choir blazes through to the end with no hint of any rallentando.

16 God is good
If organ accompaniment is used, the player may choose to omit alternate semiquavers in the bass. This will not detract from the rhythmic impulse in any way. There must be no hint of a pause if the optional ending is used.

17 Hallelujah, my Father
Always thoughtful. "Know-ing" and other similar words need a sustained, gentle second syllable. The descant may be sung immediately or saved for a repeat of the whole song.

18 Holy, holy, holy
The song flows serenely. The two syllables of the syncopated word "be-fore" must not be hurried. The Unison section at Bar 19 makes an expansive and dignified climax.

20 Holy, holy, holy is the Lord
The song can gather strength as it goes on. The descant to verse 4 should be rhythmic, with clear second beats adding strength.

21 Holy, holy, holy, the Lord God is holy
Sustained singing, with the quavers in the accompaniment bringing movement which supports the smoothness and serenity of the song.

22 I am the Bread of Life
The confidence asked for at the start will come with rhythmic, steady singing and playing. There is a hint of a march here in both song and accompaniment.

19 I was glad
Sung as a meditation. The descants, with their F naturals and E flats, give an added flavour.

23 Jesus is King
Here again the two descants provided may be used together, sung and/or played.

25 Jesus, I worship you
Warm singing with the ends of the phrases well sustained in the main tune (especially on the word "you"): the important words, "worship", "trust", "feed" and "love" should not only be clear, but should be given time to resonate.

24 Jesus, stand among us
Resonant singing, warm and confident, with the assurance of Christ's presence breaking down all barriers.

26 Jubilate, everybody
The staccato bass part (in octaves where possible) should be strong and self-assertive.

27 Lord, have mercy on us
There is a pleasing pianissimo effect available in the keyboard part in Bars 6 and 10. The singers need to finish their phrases in time for it to be heard.

28 Lord, the light of your love
(*Shine, Jesus, shine*)
Fast enough to be enjoyable, but always with room for the meaning of the words. In every appearance of "Let there be light!", make the two Ls very strong indeed. The suggested choir ending is optional, quoting from the hymn-tune *Moscow*: here there should be no hint of any change of speed, even in the final bars.

30 Majesty
Full, glowing harmonies from the choir, and rhythmic playing from the keyboard, will make this sonorous and exciting.

31 Make me a channel
A thoughtful prayer which must never allow the words merely to 'chatter'. A little time is needed at the climax (Bars 52-54) to let the organ harmonies resonate, before dropping back once more to the prayerful refrain.

32 May the fragrance of Jesus
The antiphon between men and ladies is desirable, though not essential. The congregation (and choir) can simply sing the lower stave without the echo. The speed must allow the triplet "in adoration" to be sung without haste.

33 **Meekness and Majesty** *(This is your God)*
Always steady enough for the words to carry their meaning to both singer and listener. The accompanist may imagine the sound of a guitar thrumming. The choir chords can fill out strongly towards the end of each verse, and particularly at the very end of the song.

34 **"Moses, I know you're the man"**
An unashamedly lively bass part is the essential ingredient here.

35 **O Holy Spirit**
Flowing, with the words sitting gently on the tune and an atmosphere of serenity and devotion. The descant has an optional second part.

36 **O let the Son of God enfold you** *(Spirit Song)*
Clear, resonant words, with a lilting rhythmic feeling. The accompaniment should be discreet: the singing must have a life of its own, progressing harmonically and rhythmically, even without it.

37 **Restore, O Lord**
The words "liv-ing God" in each verse should have strong accentuation and the word "God" should have both length and volume. The speed should carry the quavers of the descant without rushing them.

38 **Seek ye first the kingdom of God**
The speed must allow the words to be steady and thoughtful. The accompanist may use the choir parts for verse 1, and the two keyboard parts, with more sonority and less detail, for subsequent verses. These are suggestions only. The choir ending is optional: the accompanist may choose to play the last few choir notes, or to wait until the final chord.

40 **Sing alleluia to the Lord**
There is plenty of energy to be unleashed here. The song may be sung in Unison throughout, or with the singers divided into two parts. Men and women are suggested here, but two parts from two sides of a church would work well.

41 **Sovereign Lord**
The first verse may be sung in Unison. The optional choir parts for verse 2 make a choir descant: the soprano part may be used as a single line instrument.

29 **Spirit of the living God**
The first verse may be repeated at the end of the song. At the opening, or on this repeat, it may be sung by a soprano solo, or by a tenor and soprano together, above humming accompaniment.

42 **Such love**
The meaning of the words must come first in the minds of the singers, emphasising the devotional aspect of the song. Keep the triplets restful.

43 **Take this bread (i)**
The opening phrase should sit serenely on the gentle, swaying accompaniment. The words of the verses must be sung clearly. There is an echo effect in "Take it" and similar places: This optional echo part may be sung by the whole choir, by a part of it, or by a group of people placed away from the main body of singers.

44 **Take this bread (ii)**
Devout, with the notes always filled out with gentle sound.

45 **Thank you, Jesus**
Always gentle and thoughtful, bringing out the meaning of the words.

46 **Thank you, Lord**
Buoyant and bright, with the sound of the words making a strong rhythmic contribution.

39 **There is a Redeemer**
Expansive, confident and thankful.

47 **We are here to praise you**
The speed is governed by the first words, which must run easily and calmly. The words "sing", "bring", "love" and "hearts" need well-sustained, resonant singing.

48 **When I look into your Holiness**
The song must be slow enough to allow Bar 7 to sound relaxed. The singing of "found the joy" (Bar 10) must have enough 'give and take' for the words to be heard.

49 **With my heart I worship you**
Smooth singing with gentle movement and glowing chords. The descant singers for verse 3 may be placed away from the main group.

50 **You are the King of glory**
There should be a steady marching feeling, coupled with a really full sound on "Glory in the highest heaven", and strong affirmation of "Jesus the Messiah reigns".

51 **You have changed my sadness**
A strong rhythmic beat should come from both singers and accompaniment. The staccato bass, whether on piano or organ, will help the voices to sound jubilant and excited.

52 **You shall go out with joy**
(The trees of the field)
The rhythmic vitality relies on a strong bass accompaniment and energetic singing.